YOU CHOOSE
IF YOU LIVE OR DIE

JUNGLE CRASH

SIMON CHAPMAN

LONDON·SYDNEY

First published in 2013
by Franklin Watts

Text © Simon Chapman 2013
Illustrations by David Cousens © Franklin Watts 2013

Franklin Watts
338 Euston Road
London NW1 3BH

Franklin Watts Australia
Level 17/207 Kent Street
Sydney, NSW 2000

A CIP catalogue record for this book
is available from the British Library.

(pb) ISBN: 978 1 4451 1362 3
(Library ebook) ISBN: 978 1 4451 2563 3
(ebook) 978 1 4451 1366 1

1 3 5 7 9 10 8 6 4 2

Printed in Great Britain

Franklin Watts is a division of Hachette Children's Books,
an Hachette UK company.
www.hachette.co.uk

This book is not like others you may have read. YOU will decide if you live or die by making choices that affect how the adventure unfolds.

Each section of this book is numbered. At the end of most sections, you will have to make a choice. The choice you make will take you to a different section of the book.

Some of your choices will help you to survive the adventure. But choose carefully! The wrong decisions could cost you your life...

If you die, then go back to the chapter number you are given and learn from your mistake.

If you choose correctly, you will survive.

CHAPTER ONE

You're on board a light aircraft when it suddenly banks hard left. You instantly know something is wrong. Your stomach lurches and all you can see out of the port-side window is pure dark-green jungle; the treetops look like broccoli from this altitude. The winding, brown river that was there is now out of sight. There's no obvious reason why the plane turned: no storm, no emergency alarm. No, the pilot changed course on purpose. From the way he is studying the map that the smartly dressed man next to him clipped to the instrument panel, you suspect he intended to make this course change all along.

You turn round. The passenger sitting on the seat behind you — who you nicknamed "Worried Man" — is fumbling for something inside a black bag on his lap. He brushes his

sweaty hair out of his face before pulling
a gun from the bag. He doesn't even look
at you. Instead, he leans forward over you,
trying to attract the pilot's attention.

"Piloto!" he shouts over the thrum of the
engine. "Señor!"

You nudge Ramiro, the man you are

travelling with. He is sleeping in a seat next to you. He works on a zoological project with your sister at the Tambopata National Reserve, near Puerto Maldonado, which is where you're supposed to be going.

Worried Man talks to the pilot in Spanish — he's asking why the pilot has changed direction. As Ramiro wakes up, you catch his eyes and slide your gaze over towards Worried Man. The expression on Ramiro's face freezes when he sees the man's gun. "Dios," he mouths. "Cocaleros." Ramiro thinks Worried Man is a drug runner!

"Girar el plano de todo!" Worried Man shouts. He pushes his gun into the back of the pilot's head.

"If you kill the pilot, then we all die," the man next to the pilot says.

You had assumed he was the co-pilot, but now you realise his expensive shades and designer shirt aren't what a pilot would wear. And now you think about it, he had been the one who put the map on the instrument panel. The co-pilot swings round, pointing a large handgun at Worried Man. "Suelte el arma," he says calmly.

Worried Man pauses, as though making his choice. Bang! The co-pilot shoots him before he can move. You duck down as another shot, and then another are fired. The aircraft's windscreen shatters, and the propellor blasts the cockpit with air. There's another shot fired before Worried Man drops down across the seats — no longer worried, just dead. Ramiro glances across at you as the plane lurches downwards. You sit up slowly, gripping the seat in front. The pilot is slumped across the controls — dead. The co-pilot — or whoever he is — has blood pouring from his face and hands, and is either dead or unconscious. His gun has gone.

"Can you fly?" you ask Ramiro over the

noise of the wind and engine.

"No. No. Can you?" he asks, already knowing what the answer will be.

Without hesitating, you push between the seats.

Survival Challenge: Descent into the jungle

Of course you haven't ever flown a real plane, but that's not going to stop you trying! The plane is already diving towards the forest below, its engine straining as the revs increase. You doubt if you can stop the plane crashing, but you can prevent yourself and Ramiro dying.

You pull the dead pilot to one side and grasp the control yoke. You can use this like a steering wheel to move the aircraft left and right, but also to climb or dive. You also spot what you are certain is the throttle lever.

The decisions you make now will decide whether you live or die.

➜   If you want to throttle the engine "up" for more power, go to 77.

➜   If you want to throttle the engine "down" for less power, go to 90.

➜   If you wish to pull the control yoke towards you, go to 36.

1.

You turn and move out of the water along the stream, tracing the flow of the water upstream. Slowly you realise you are moving round and back into the swamp.

➜   To continue upstream, go to 52.

➜   To go turn back, and follow the water downstream, go to 66.

2.

You strike the wasps' nest and it falls to the ground. Wasps swarm out as you run past. Seconds later, the man chasing you runs right into the angry insects. You hear him

1

2

cry out as he is stung dozens of times. You can hear him cursing and crashing around in the undergrowth. You decide now is a good time to head for the tree with the sticky red sap. Go to 64.

3.

You begin to head back to Ramiro. You are just pushing through a clump of big-leaved plants when you see a man wearing a floppy bush hat. He's possibly from a forest tribe, and is crouched over your footprints! He is carrying a homemade-looking rifle. On seeing you, the man hollers, "Buen día!" You notice that, while his face is smiling and his left hand is held up in greeting, his right hand is pointing the rifle towards you.

➜   To stop and greet the man, go to 58.

➜   To run back into the undergrowth, go to 85.

4.

You duck into the long grass and chase after the man. Without really thinking, you

barge into him. As he falls down, he presses the "fire" button and the rocket streaks away. It narrowly misses one of the two helicopters and explodes one of the high trees across from the airstrip. The flames light up figures in dark commando-style gear jumping down from a helicopter. The guard curses, "Te mato!" before he starts to pull a handgun from his belt.

➜ If you have the spade, go to 76.

➜ If you do not have the spade, go to 32.

5.

You veer off to the right into the thicker undergrowth where it is darker. It slows you down, but it also slows down the man behind you. "Stop there you little runt," Pedro curses. He shines the torch towards you, and slashes wildy at the leaves with a machete.

➜ To stop and fight Pedro, go to 74.

➜ To duck out of the way and keep on running, go to 22.

6.

Before you can move, you hear a gunshot from the direction in which you left Ramiro. The men start running towards the sound. You run back the way you came. When you reach the stream, Ramiro is on his feet. He's propped up by a man wearing a floppy bush hat. They are still on the opposite side of the water, but you can clearly see the man has a rifle. The other three men are now approaching.

➜ If you wish to stay hidden and wait to

see what happens, go to 75.

➜ If you'd prefer to walk out from your hiding place, go to 50.

7.

You dig the end of your pole deep into the riverbed and push the raft around into the shallow water. Enrico's boat cannot follow you here, and it swings round to avoid the gravel. You duck down as Enrico opens fire with an AK47. The noise is terrifying. Pedro turns their boat for another pass.

➜ To run the raft aground on the gravel, and run into the forest, go to 35.

➜ To turn back towards the channel and attempt to ride the rapids further down, go to 94.

8.

You grab another vine, but as soon as you place weight on it the whole thing comes away, and you plummet downwards. You hear Ramiro call out above you, but there's nothing he can do. Your screams are cut off as you hit the rocks below.

➡ You've fallen to your death. Get back to Chapter 2.

9.

You don't have enough power to make this manoeuvre! For an instant, the plane hangs in the air, then the nose dips and you dive into the forest below.

➡ You've crashed in the jungle and been killed. What a letdown! Get back to Chapter 1 to try again.

10.

You cut the rope and the camouflage net falls down on the guards. Before they have a chance to untangle themselves, you grab the spade and run over to the men. Neither of them has a chance as you strike them with the spade. With both guards knocked out, you are about to get back behind the shed, when a man carrying an RPG comes out of the darkness. The cocaleros have a rocket-propelled grenade launcher!

➜ If you want to carry out Plan A, and set fire to the shed, go to 28.

➜ If you want to chase after the man holding the RPG, go to 4.

➜ If you want to take cover behind some nearby containers, go to 92.

11.

Enrico levels his gun at you and fires. The bullets rake across the raft hitting both you and Ramiro. You slump down onto the gravel beach, which is to be your final resting place.

➜ You are dead — go back to Chapter 5.

12.

After a quick search the man finds the map and phone. "Ah, thank you," he says. He flicks a glance at one of his men — an instruction of some kind. You don't see the man behind you raise his rifle, nor do you feel any pain as the bullets cut you down.

➜   You've been killed. Go back to Chapter 3 to try the challenge again.

13.

You push through the webs and they cling to your arms, face and hair. You try to wipe them away, but Enrico's man is catching up fast! You need to make a snap decision.

➜   To head over to the left, go to 62.

➜   To carry on forward, go to 84.

14.

You aim for the thin trees.

"Hold on!" you shout to Ramiro before bracing yourself for the impact.

Vines stretch and snap as the plane ploughs through them. Metal screeches as a wing is ripped off, and as branches smash and scrape down the plane's fuselage. It seems as though you'll never stop until suddenly you jolt to a halt. But before you can take a breath, a vine holding the plane up snaps, lurching you down the short distance to the ground. You are too stunned to fully realise that you survived, or to notice the slick of warm blood seeping from a gash in your forehead before you pass out.

CHAPTER TWO

When you wake up, your head is pounding and one of your eyes is stuck shut with blood. It is still light, that much you can see. You unfasten your harness and quickly check for any injuries. You have a cut on your head and some scratches on your arms, but you're alive! The pilot wasn't so lucky. A check of his pulse tells you he's long dead, and the co-pilot with the designer clothing is too. The Worried Man is nowhere to be seen, but Ramiro is lying squashed between the back seats. His leg is bent back at an unnatural angle, but at least he's breathing. You drag him out and prop him up away from the plane.

The first thing that strikes you about the rainforest is the steamy heat. The sun, obscured by leaves and branches, is high in the sky. Flies and tiny bees are buzzing around the corpses.

You go back over to the plane to see what you can salvage. You grab half a packet of biscuits and a plastic water bottle from the pocket behind the co-pilot's seat. In his expensive-looking jacket you find a lighter, a folding knife and a satellite phone. The display is cracked and the battery compartment is partly open. When you click it into place, the yellow screen lights up: "no signal — charge low". You switch the phone off. You search for the man's gun, but when you can't find it you remember Worried Man had one too. It's under one of the seats, covered in blood. When you finally manage to open it you're disappointed there aren't any bullets left — it might have been handy. You cast it aside. In the back of the plane you find a zip-up sports bag. It has lots of plastic packets inside containing gritty, white powder which you guess could be drugs or chemicals to process them. You discard the packets, but keep the bag.

Then under some leaves you find the co-pilot's map. It is large scale with various labels in Spanish, rivers and numbers. There's a name you recognise: Puerto Maldonado. It's the town where your sister is based. If you can work out where you are, maybe you'll be able to get to her after all.

Ramiro groans loudly as he comes round. You go over and give him some water. His breathing is laboured and it's clear he's in a lot of pain.

"I think the plane was being used to transport drugs," you say, and tell him

about what you've found. He doesn't look surprised.

"We must leave here," he says, grasping at your T-shirt. "Those packets were probably destined for a drug processing factory. Cocaine, you know?" Ramiro struggles to get to his feet. You grab a broken branch he can use to support himself.

"The stuff on the plane is valuable enough for the cocaleros to come looking for it. So is that map and phone. My guess is that it shows the location of their drugs factories. If the police or army had it, then their operation here would be over. Come, collect your things."

"Shouldn't we stay here and wait to be rescued?" you ask. "Hasn't this plane got some sort of black box transponder that will send out our location? We could call someone with the satellite phone. "

Ramiro looks at you as if you are an

idiot. "On a plane like this? I think you must have hit your head really hard!" he chuckles. "We're off any flight route. If this wreck gets found then it will be by the cocaleros, and they'll kill us."

"But your leg? Is it broken?" you point out.

"I will take my chances. I would rather try to get out than be shot by cocaleros or starve to death here."

Survival Challenge: Setting off

An hour later you've splinted Ramiro's leg and tied it up with strips of seat covering. "The phone is useless here," Ramiro says. "Under the forest canopy we may get a text message out of it, but we need a good clear view of the sky. Plus, we don't even know where we are. We have to get to a big river."

You sling the zip-up bag across your back and wade towards across the marshy ground. You can see Ramiro is suffering, and every step is a challenge.

Soon you are up to your knees in muddy water. The air is filled with the whining of mosquitoes and the cackling calls of unseen birds in the vegetation around you. Something just moved in the water nearby; a crocodile or an anaconda perhaps?

The decisions you make now will decide whether you live or die.

➜   If you want to carry on forwards towards the tall trees you can see ahead, go to 87.
➜   If you would rather persuade Ramiro to head back to the plane wreck, go to 27.

15.
You press on, but you are lost by the time it gets dark. You get little sleep during the hot, wet and insect-ridden night. In the morning you can hardly open your eyes because their lids have been so bitten

by mosquitoes. You stumble around with Ramiro for three more days. On the fifth day you can't wake him. Two days later, with your head wound infected, you stumble face down into mud and never get up.

➜   Pick yourself up and get back to Chapter 2.

16.

The trees below are frighteningly close and you are still going very fast. Quickly you strap yourself in and cut the power to the overheating engine.

➜   If you decide to aim for a small patch of open water towards the middle of the swamp, go to 29.

➜   If you wish to aim for the thin trees and vines by the swamp edge, go to 14.

➜   If you wish to aim for the taller trees past the swamp, go to 60.

17.

You hardly have time to register what happens next. You struggle to stay surfaced, but the raft swings round, slamming you into a large boulder. The wind is knocked out of you. You sink beneath the bubbling river.

➜ You are dead. Go back to Chapter 5.

18.

You run, but just when you think you've got away, there's a loud crack. Your back sears with a burning pain. You stumble on for a few more steps before you pitch face down. All you can think about are those pretty yellow butterflies as your vision fades to black.

➜ You are dead. Get back to Chapter 3.

19.

You decide to climb up and over the tree, but it's tough going. You clamber through the fallen tree branches, and pull Ramiro up after you. He is clearly in a lot of pain. You are stung by several wasps as you clamber along, but you both make it to the other side of the tree. Go to 46.

20.

You choose Plan B, and quickly set fire
to the torch with your lighter. You move
out from the undergrowth and wave the
flaming torch, hoping that the helicopters
will see it. Unfortunately they're not the
first ones to spot you — the cocaleros are.
Soon bullets are buzzing over your head.

➡   If you decide to drop the torch, head
back into the undergrowth, and go with
Plan A, go to 34.

➡   If you decide to continue waving your
torch, go to 91.

➡   If you want to drop the torch, run
to the other side of the camp, and hide
behind a tent, go to 48.

21.

You press the engine cutoff. You continue
to dive down towards the forest, wind
whistling in your ears. You hear Ramiro
scream as you hit the trees. Branches
splinter as the plane smashes through
the thick canopy until you finally come

to a halt. You're just about to celebrate surviving when the plane lurches downwards again. The plane buckles as it hits the ground. Neither you or Ramiro make it out alive.

➜   Go back to Chapter 1, and next time find a better place to land!

22.

You duck down and under a low-hanging branch. Pedro's machete swings over your head and embeds in the hard wood. You take a sharp turn and push through the vegetation that will take you past the spider webs and back onto yesterday's trail.

➜   If you want to head over to a large buttress root, go to 62.

➜   If you want to carry on forward towards a spiky tree trunk, go to 84.

23.

You pull back some leaves and find a snake right in front of your face. You can only see part of its diamond-patterned body and head.

➜ To quickly stab the snake with your knife, go to 69.

➜ To stay very still, go to 81.

24.

You move further round behind the containers. You take out your folding knife and stab a hole in the bottom of one. Liquid that smells like fuel begins to pour out. You back away slowly, and when the armed men appear, you flick the lighter and toss it at the containers. The reaction is explosive, and the men are engulfed in flames. Suddenly there's the roar of an engine starting up and a twin-prop light aircraft bursts out of the palm-thatched shed. It has to be Enrico trying to escape! There is nothing you can do but stand and watch. It's then that you notice a dead man lying at your feet — it's the guard who had the RPG. You can't see any rockets,

but he has a handgun in his belt. You grab
the gun just as a man dressed all in black
jogs up to you.

➜ To shoot at the figure, go to 67.

➜ Drop the gun and hold your hands up,
go to 101.

25.

You drop the map and phone and step forwards. "I can't believe it. Is it really you," the leader says in English. He laughs with surprise. One of the men speaks rapidly to him in Spanish. He points to where you have just dropped the map and satellite phone. Go to 12.

26.

You ignore Enrico behind you and turn to steer down the rapids. You don't get very far before he opens fire again, this time catching you in the back. You twist round in agony, losing your balance, and tumble into the foamy water. Go to 44.

27.

Ramiro doesn't like your decision, but he's not in a position to argue. You turn around and head back, but soon you're not sure which direction you've come from. Your view in all directions is green leaves, tree trunks, vines and muddy water. Go to 15.

25

26

27

28.

You head behind the shed to set fire to the dry grass. The fire soon spreads up the side of the shed. But the burning smell hasn't gone unnoticed. A guard dog appears out of the smoke and launches itself at you, knocking you backwards. As you attempt to get up a gunshot rings in your ears, and you tumble back into the grass, dead.

➜ Get back to Chapter 6.

29.

You aim for the middle of the swamp.

"Hold on!" you scream.

Wind rushes through your hair as the plane hits the surface. The aircraft snags on something under the water and flips upside down. Mud pours in through the smashed windscreen. There is no time to catch your breath as you and Ramiro sink into the swamp, never to be seen again.

➜ Fly back to Chapter 1 to try again.

30.

You push ahead but your foot snags on a root and you crash to the ground. The man behind you sees his opportunity and dives onto you, cracking you on the back of the head. You pass out. Go to 45.

31.

You creep forward slowly using low spreading palm trees for cover. As you come up to the lighthouse tree, you see two scruffy-looking men armed with automatic rifles taking pot shots at the monkeys. A third man, more neatly dressed, stands watching. He looks like the leader, and is a younger version of the co-pilot — the man whose dead body you left at the crash site! You realise these men must be cocaleros — drug runners. They are probably looking for the plane!

➜   If you want to risk hiding the co-pilot's map and satellite phone, go to 98.

➜   If you want to keep hold of the map

and phone, and get back to Ramiro as quickly as you can, go to 6.

➜ To keep hold of the map and phone, and walk out to greet the men, go to 50.

32.

Before you can react you're shot and you fall to your kness, clutching your stomach. You die, alone in the darkness, before the rescue team can reach you.

➜ Go back to Chapter 6.

33.

Ahead of you, masses of yellow butterflies flutter around a strip of sand at the water's edge. You help Ramiro down, guiding him on the best path to the bottom.

He arrives, sweating heavily. He smiles when he catches sight of the golden patch of sand.

"We'll camp here," he says.

CHAPTER THREE

Night falls quickly in the rainforest and, apart from a few stars glimpsed through gaps in the treetops, the blackness is complete. Tree frogs trill out their calls, bats flutter close by and unseen animals rustle through the vegetation behind your strip of sand.

You and Ramiro were so tired that you

fell asleep virtually as soon as you stopped. Now that you're awake it's chilly, and you're regretting not gathering some wood and getting a fire going. You nibble one of the biscuits, wrap your arms around your body and sit it out. It's going to be a long night.

Morning. Everything is damp with dew. There are green parakeets flying overhead and a roaring noise that you hope might be an aircraft coming to look for you. Then you realise that it's actually howler monkeys. You feel hungry and miserable, so you make a list to help you focus. Get a fire going. Warm up. Eat some food. If you're going to survive then you decide that you must start thinking like a survivor.

You gather up some sticks, which Ramiro tells you are balsawood, and these catch fire easily. There are animal tracks in the soft sand all around your camp, and you are sure most weren't there yesterday afternoon when you arrived. Some are three-toed hoof prints of what Ramiro tells you is probably a tapir. Others are large, four-toed and without claw marks; like a cat, perhaps a jaguar. Some of its tracks follow scrape-marks in the sand, and there are shallow holes where it dug down. In one of the holes you notice something white, and a little digging reveals what look like five ping-pong balls.

"Good. Those are turtle eggs," Ramiro says. "Put them at the edge of the fire. All we need now is some bacon!" he jokes.

The warm yolks go down a treat; it feels good having food in your stomach at last. You head off on foot down the bank of the stream.

Soon you're into a routine of walking along the river bars, crossing to the other side each time the stream turns. It's slow going with Ramiro injured and, as the day wears on, you have to support him more and more.

"I need to rest," he says. "Scout ahead as far as that lighthouse tree." He points to a huge tree with spreading branches at the next bend in the stream. "I have a feeling we might find a larger river there. Those birds are red-faced caracaras, and they don't live in deep forest."

You kneel down next to a pool slightly

separated from the main stream and go to fill your water bottle. "Hey, wait. Don't fill up the bottle from there," Ramiro warns you. "I've just seen an electric eel surface. One hundred and twenty volts. That's enough to knock you out! Go to the tree, see if you can find the river. Look for people fishing, or smoke coming from fires. Take the map and phone," he says, "but don't use the phone until we are sure of our location. Don't forget it may only have enough charge for one call."

Survival Challenge: At the lighthouse tree

You leave your bag behind and head off towards the lighthouse tree, using your surroundings to help make a mental note of the direction you are moving in. You can see the spindly, black shapes of spider monkeys in the treetops. Several are making loud coughing sounds, when the air resounds with the crack of a rifle shot that nearly makes you drop the map and phone.

The noise of the rifle can mean only one thing: there are people here!

The decisions you make now will decide whether you live or die.

➡   To run forward before the people have a chance to move on, go to 50.

➡   To creep forward slowly in the bushes at the edge of the forest, go to 31.

➡   If you think it could be too dangerous, and wish to head back to where you left Ramiro, go to 3.

34.

You choose Plan A, and move as fast as you can along the hidden trail. The men in the camp are preparing for an attack, and with all the shouting and the thud of the approaching helicopters you are able to sneak right up to the side of the large shed. You are about to use some tinder to start a fire, when you notice two men setting up what looks like a heavy machine gun.

➡ If you want to carry on with your plan, and set fire to the shed, go to 28.

➡ If you want to look for a way to take out the guards and the heavy machine gun, go to 51.

35.
You use the pole to push the raft over towards the gravel. It becomes stuck and you jump down into the shallow water. You turn to lift Ramiro off, when gunfire from

Enrico's boat peppers the wooden raft. You desperately try to pull Ramiro off, but the last of your strength is gone. Go to 11.

36.

You pull back the control yoke and the nose of the plane rises. You've levelled out and stopped the dive, but several red lights are flashing on the instrument panel.

"I think the shooting damaged the plane!" you shout at Ramiro.

"Then we need to find somewhere to land, before we crash!" he replies.

You bank the plane round just as an alarm buzzes in the cockpit. Go to 47.

37.

You stumble around looking for a stick to flick the spider away, when you hear someone splashing through the water behind you. A powerful torch beam falls on you. You snatch up a stick and flick the spider away. Now in the torchlight you can see there are lots of spider webs slung across ahead of you. "Alto ahí!" the man shouts behind you.

➜ To push straight through the spider webs you'll have to take a chance. Go to either 13 or 30.

➜ To find a way around them, go to 5.

38.

You keep the raft close to the bank and away from the raging river. But soon you realise that the water here is too shallow, and the logs of the raft catch on the riverbed. You jump off onto a rock to pull the raft through. Without your weight the logs float higher in the water and it works!

➜ If you want to push the raft back into the flow using your hands, go to 70.

➜ To get back on and push off on the rock using the pole, go to 89.

39.

You decide to continue to follow the

stream. The mud is slippery, and you soon find wading in the water is the easiest option. Then you turn a sharp bend to find your way blocked by a large fallen tree.

➜ If you want to climb up and over the tree trunk, go to 19.

➜ If you wish to crawl under the trunk, go to 23.

➜ If you decide to go back the way you came and climb up to the higher ground to the side of the stream, go to 95.

40.

Your shot goes wide, obliterating the shed but missing Enrico's plane, which has reached the airstrip. The plane accelerates and escapes. As you watch, one of Enrico's guards grabs you from behind you and seconds later you are dead.

➜ Go back to Chapter 6.

41.

You run along the trail, and straight past

the wasps' nest. But as you move you can hear someone behind you. Enrico's man has caught up with you!

➜ To sneak off the trail and hide, hoping that Enrico's man will run past, go to 68.

➜ To keep running along the rough trail, go to 30.

42.

You look around for another way to take out the guards. You spot that the camouflage netting above them is held up by a rope tied to two pegs nearby.

➜ To cut the rope with your folding knife and wait to see what happens, go to 100.

➜ To cut the rope with your knife and then grab the spade, go to 10.

43.

None of the men look friendly, in fact they seem pretty fed up. Three are carrying automatic rifles that look like AK47s. The fourth has a face like a younger version of the co-pilot — the man you left dead at the plane crash site. This man is clearly the leader. Seeing his face reminds you that you are carrying the dead man's satellite phone and map, the one with the drugs factories marked on it.

➜   If you want to risk dropping the map and phone in the undergrowth by the lighthouse tree, go to 63.

➜   If you decide to keep the map and phone, and greet the men as they approach, go to 50.

➜   If you'd rather run away now while there may be a chance, go to 18.

44.

Your body is pulled down and spins over as the power of the water sucks you down. You don't have the strength to fight a river, and when you run out of air, you simply let the current take you away.

➜   Go back to Chapter 5.

45.

You wake up back at the site of the plane crash to the stink of rotting meat. Enrico is angry — very angry. He threatens to shoot you unless you tell him exactly where the map and phone are. When you refuse, and he puts a bullet through your leg, you finally tell him. Then he shoots you anyway.

➜   You are dead. Get back to Chapter 4 to put a stop to Enrico's plans.

46.

You and Ramiro head towards the sound of crashing water. You arrive where the stream plunges over a waterfall. You look out over the edge. There are vines, rocks and a pool below.

"It's too high to jump," you tell Ramiro.

"I don't have the energy to walk round," he replies. You decide the only thing to do is to climb down the rocks using the vines.

➜   You're going to need a little bit of luck to survive this. Choose either 99 or 56.

47.

A flashing red light has appeared on the engine temperature readout. The engine is overheating!

"This isn't good!" you shout.

Then something catches your eye. There is a lighter green patch of forest ahead, where the trees are spread more thinly. You could attempt to land there.

➔ If you wish to attempt a landing in the area where there are fewer trees, go to 55.

➔ If you'd rather turn the plane to try to find the river, go to 82.

48.

You drop the torch as more of the cocaleros open fire. Shots fill the air around you, but you manage to duck into the long grass and then to sprint across the airstrip. Just as you are getting close to the camp, a heavy machine gun opens fire.

➔ You'll only survive this by luck — choose either 83 or 32.

49.

You can sense this man is dangerous, and you don't think telling him about the map and phone will be a good idea. "I took some water and a lighter. There was nothing else," you lie. He looks at you, but you hold his stare. "OK. Okay. You will take me back to the plane, sí?" the leader says. His tone is friendly, but you sense this is an order, not a question. A man in a floppy hat and carrying a home-made rifle steps out of the jungle, pulling Ramiro along with him. He has your bag, and when the leader looks at him, he just shakes his head.

CHAPTER FOUR

The leader, Enrico, explains that he runs a business in the jungle with his brother, Emilio.

"Sorry we alarmed you," he says. "I worried when my brother's plane did not arrive. And now I think maybe he is dead."

You glance across the driftwood fire that has been started. Ramiro is sitting between Mamani, the tribal man with the floppy hat, and a man called Carlos, who is busy cooking some meat Mamani has caught. The fourth man, Pedro, is off in the bush taking a leak.

"That is why you must take us back to the crash site. I must find my brother." Enrico looks at you with his steely eyes. "Don't worry about your friend. I will leave Carlos with him. Then, when we're back, we'll take you both out on my boat."

Carlos hands you a bowl of steaming-hot rice and grisly meat, which you find out is peccary. You're glad of the drinking water and food, but something about this just doesn't seem right. They've taken your lighter and the folding knife they found.

And you're sure they've been deliberately keeping you and Ramiro apart. It's only when the four men are laughing and joking together that you and Ramiro get a chance to talk.

"It's the phone," Ramiro whispers. "I heard Carlos talking about earlier. It has information, important numbers. You do know where it is, don't you?"

"I hope so," you admit.

"When they split up you must escape from Enrico and the other two, and meet me back here. I can take care of Carlos..." His eyes slide towards the pool where he pointed out the electric eel earlier. "Then we can get the map and phone and get out of here alive."

You stop talking as Carlos comes over. He says something that sounds like a threat, and then pokes Ramiro's injured leg with his foot.

Your friend grimaces. "You need to go now," he says. "Good luck."

The way back along the stream takes much less time than when you came the other way with Ramiro. Mamani turns out to be Enrico's lead guide. He finds an easy route that cuts out the stream's twisty meanders — it's clear that he is an expert in the rainforest. Escaping from the others would be easy, but not Mamani. He would have no problem tracking you. You have to get rid of him or get him on your side. So, as you walk behind him, stepping where he does, you devise a plan. You remember a kidnap movie you saw once. When people are held captive they say to make your captors get to know you. If they realise you are a real person with a home life and a family, they are less likely to kill you. You decide to try this on Mamani. While you're ahead of the others you start by telling Mamani your name, but he simply takes no notice. It's only when you pull out a photo of your sister and her co-workers at Puerto Maldonado, that he seems interested. He snatches the picture from your hand and pushes you away, his finger outlining the people, his lips mumbling names.

You reach over his arms and point to the long-haired young woman. "That's my sister."

Mamani stares hard at you, pockets the picture then carries on his way. There is no more contact after that but you do notice how, from now on, each time your route changes he takes time to stare at each point of interest; a uniquely twisted vine, a line of bright red sticky sap oozing from a tree trunk, a wasps' nest, and an enormous buttress root. To him, these are landmarks to find the way, and he's making you memorise them too.

By late afternoon you've reached the edge of the swamp where the plane wreck lies. Mamani points out some broken undergrowth.

"The plane is through there somewhere, but there's nowhere to camp," you say. You arc right, it will be dark soon, but you also don't want Enrico to arrive and find out that his dead brother's map and phone are missing.

Enrico looks to Mamani who responds softly and points to the sky.

"We make camp back there," he orders.

Survival Challenge: Escape from Enrico

You spend the night in a hammock under a blue plastic tarpaulin that Enrico's men sling up across a gap between two trees. The others have mosquito nets, except for you and Mamani. He tossed an old termite nest onto the campfire, which made a sweet-smelling smoke that kept the insects away.

You are woken before dawn. Mamani is shaking you. His hand is over your mouth to stop you crying out. He places your folding knife and lighter into your hand, and gestures for you to go.

The decisions you make now will decide whether you live or die.

You don't have time to thank Mamani. You move as quickly and as silently as you can. Suddenly you hear shouts from behind you. You're so busy looking for your first landmark — the buttress root — in the early morning light, that you run forward and get a face full of spider. It's large, black-and-yellow and now it's sitting on your shoulder!

➜　To brush it off with your hand and carry on, go to 54.

➜　To reach down for a stick to get the spider off without touching it, go to 37.

50.

"Hi, there!" you say.

The leader takes a close look at you and laughs with surprise. "I can't believe it. Is it really you?" he says in English. "You were on the plane with Emilio, my brother, sí? You know, the man with the smart clothes, smart hair." The man looks around. "But I don't see him here. Where is he?"

You hesitate. You don't know how the man will react if he knows his brother is dead. So you do the only thing you can, stall him.

"I don't know. The plane ... the crash. It was a mess," you tell the leader.

"That's OK," he says placing his hand on your shoulder. "You're alive. You are going to help me find him. But first I need to know if you have … taken … anything. From the plane."

➡ If you still have the map and phone, go to 12.

➡ If you do not have them, go to 49.

51.

The heavy machine gun could easily shoot down the helicopters. But there are two guards, and even if you were feeling 100 per cent it would be tough. So, you look around for something to help you.

➡ To grab a spade leaning up against the shed and use it to attack the men, go to 79.

➡ If you want to look for another way to overpower the men first, go to 42.

52.

You continue to follow the water upstream, but the ground becomes swampy again.

Soon you're chest deep in water, with Ramiro struggling to put one foot in front of the other. It's not long before one part of the forest looks very much like another. Go to 15.

53.

You line up the raft in the middle, ready to run the rapids. The river funnels into a foaming torrent between two car-sized boulders. "Get ready!" you scream at Ramiro as a bullet whizzes over your head. You turn to see Enrico lining up another shot.

➡️   To steer down the rapids, go to 26.

➡️   To crouch down and steer down the rapids, go to 61.

➡️   To lie flat on the raft like Ramiro, and cling on, go to 78.

54.

You quickly swat the spider away with the back of your hand. You can hear one of Enrico's men splashing about with a torch behind you. The beam lights up dozens of webs which stretch across in front of you.

→ To walk around the webs that criss-cross the trail from yesterday, go to 5.

→ If you want to go straight through the webs, go to 13.

→ If you'd prefer to go on hands and knees under the webs, go to 97.

55.

You're flying towards the clearing and slowly begin to reduce the throttle. Below, thin, wispy trees stick up from a mass of reeds and bamboo. You see water reflecting beneath the vegetation. This is a swamp. "Are you sure about this?" Ramiro shouts.

→ To carry on your course in an attempt to land, go to 16.

→ To push forward on the throttle and climb up to find somewhere else, go to 96.

56.

You begin to climb down the rocks, using

the vines like a rope to help you. Ants
crawl out and over your hands and up your
arms, but you can do nothing but ignore
them. You slip on several occasions, but
you reach the bottom of the waterfall
safely. Go to 33.

57.

You push left into the swirling water, but it
brings you to a complete stop, and instead
spins the raft around. You are caught in a
powerful eddy!

➜ To use the pole to push the raft out of
the eddy, back into the rapids, go to 72.

➜ To jump off the raft into the water
and attempt to push the raft yourself, go
to 44.

58.

The man looks friendly enough, so you step
forward. "Am I glad to see—" but before
you can continue the man shouts "Don
Enrico, por aqui!" then he shoots into the

air. Three men arrive soon after. One of them looks like the co-pilot from the plane. Go to 12.

59.
You wake — your whole body aches. Enrico is standing over you with a terrible grin on his face. You are now his hostage!

➜   Go back to Chapter 6 to put a stop to his operation.

60.
You think that levelling out across the swamp and heading for the trees is the best plan. But as you get closer to the trees you realise your mistake — they're huge! The massive impact kills both you and Ramiro instantly.

➜   Get your act together, and get back to Chapter 1 to try again.

61.
You crouch down and use the pole to

control the raft. The water carries your raft forwards, speeding you between giant boulders.

➜ To use the pole to steer the raft left towards calmer, swirling water, go to 57.

➜ To push right with the pole and continue down the rapids, go to 72.

62.

This way leads to a buttress root — it's the one you recognise from yesterday! You look for the path into the forest, and easily find it where Pedro and Enrico have trampled a plant with glossy leaves. You remember that there was a wasps' nest somewhere along here.

➜ To run along the trail past the wasps' nest, go to 41.

➜ To run along the trail and hit the wasps' nest as you go past, go to 2.

63.

You decide you don't want to be caught

62

63

holding the map and phone. Since only your head and shoulders are higher than the large leaves of the undergrowth, you might be able to drop them where you're standing without anyone seeing. A better place would be in the roots of a spiny palm tree over to your right, but you'll have to walk over to it.

➜ If you decide to take a chance, and drop the map and phone where you are, go to 25.

➜ If you think it's worth risking walking over to drop the map and phone by the roots of the palm tree, go to 88.

64.

You've escaped from Enrico and his men, but you don't stop. You only slow down to make sure you are on the right route after passing the tree with the sticky sap. Light rain begins to fall as the sky brightens. You keep moving, past the plaited vine, knowing you have to get back to Ramiro as quickly as possible, but without getting lost.

CHAPTER FIVE

It's midday when you get back to the place
where you left Ramiro and you're starting
to feel weak from the lack of water, food
and sleep. It's been raining heavily and
the stream has become a raging torrent.
Carlos's body is laying face down in the
pool where Ramiro saw the electric eel.
It looks like Ramiro's plan worked, but
you can't see him anywhere. You carry on
towards the lighthouse tree, picking up
both the map and the satellite phone from
where you left them. There's still no sign
of Ramiro, so you head past the lighthouse
tree to where you hope you'll find the
larger river. You reach a riverbank where
there is a long, wooden boat pulled out of
the water. There is also a balsawood log
raft tied to a pole, which has been stuck
into the sand. Close by, two black vultures
are hopping up and down the riverbank

eyeing something lying half out of the water. It's Ramiro! You chase away the vultures and check over your friend. He's been badly beaten up.

"Ah, my friend. We go now?" he lifts his head and smiles weakly at you.

"We go," you answer. You quickly decide that you are too weak to pull the long wooden boat into the water, and also, its outboard motor is missing — Enrico must have hidden it — so you take the raft. Two minutes later you've helped Ramiro on and you're pushing off into the river's current.

The rain is easing up as you watch the lighthouse tree slowly slide out of view. You drift with the flow for the next few meanders, using the pole to help steer, when the water becomes rougher. You check on Ramiro — he is still conscious. You have nothing with you apart from the rain-soaked clothes you are wearing, the folding knife and lighter that Mamani gave back to you, and the map and phone. For the first time since the plane crash, you are in an open space. You reach into your pocket for the satellite phone — the signal is strong. There is enough charge in the battery to send a text. You don't know the emergency number, so your parents back home are your best bet. But where are you?

You study the map. You've passed a large sand bar shaped like three fingers, and there are also some large rocky outcrops as the river bends ahead. You trace similar features on the map — this must be where you are! Further downstream, the river is marked with lots of dashes, which someone had drawn a cross over. Past this there is a thick line drawn on and some GPS reference numbers; it's an airstrip! You key in the country code and your father's mobile number, then you type in your

message: "Urgent need rescue S121329 W692126 in danger friend injured". You press "send". The phone's screen flashes back "message sent".

There is some hope now. All you have to do now is get to that airstrip and wait.

The phone beeps; it flashes up "insufficient battery power for radio use", then it flashes up the "sent calls log" on the screen, and now you realise why Enrico wanted the phone so badly; these are all of his brother's contacts. There are numbers from all over the world. If the authorities had this, they could bust half the cocaine traffic in South America.

The noise of an outboard motor catches your attention. You spin round. It's too far away to tell, but you're sure it's the long wooden boat you saw at the river. It must be Enrico! You squeeze the phone into your waistband. The water has now become so rough that you have to shift your weight to stay balanced. You turn the next bend to be confronted by roaring water ahead.

Survival Challenge: The Cross on the Map

"Rapids," Ramiro mumbles, but you've seen them already. Ahead the water churns white as it crashes over rocks in the river. To the left is a high rock bank. To the right is shallower water and a gravel beach, separated from the main channel by a line of rocks that look like a dinosaur's spine, with a rainforest backdrop. Enrico's boat is closing fast from behind.

The decisions you make now will decide whether you live or die.

➜ To go down the middle of the river, and line up to ride the rapids, go to 53.

➜ If you decide to pole the raft down the shallow channel on the right, go to 7.

➜ If you want to land the raft on the gravel beach, and escape into the forest, go to 35.

65.

You pull back on the control yoke just in time. You power upwards and quickly regain control. The leaves of the trees below ripple in the wash of your propeller and there is a slight tug as the undercarriage clips the top of an emergent tree. But as you bank the plane round gently an alarm buzzes in the cockpit. Go to 47.

66.

You follow the water downstream and gradually you head further along and into

the rainforest. The stream has cut a deep gulley into the orange mud between the huge forest trees. Further along you can see a way up to higher ground.

➜ If you want to follow the narrow stream bed, go to 39.

➜ If you'd prefer to walk up onto the flatter, higher ground alongside the stream, go to 95.

67.

You shoot wildly at the figure in black and he drops down. You move cautiously over towards the body and then realise the full extent of your mistake. The body belongs to one of the Special Operations commandos sent to rescue you! But you don't have time to grieve. A bullet from the growing darkness catches you in the chest. In an instant, you are dead.

➜ Go back to Chapter 6.

68.

You step off the trail and into a bush, waiting for the man to pass by. You don't have to wait long. He charges past in the gloom, his torch doing little to help him find his way. After a while the noise of him blundering in the forest fades and you slip out. You know where to go next, so you head for the tree with the sticky red sap. Go to 64.

69.

You slowly open your knife and then lunge at the snake with your blade. The snake

strikes before you get anywhere near it.
It is a fer-de-Lance, a type of pit viper,
named for the heat-sensing pits beneath
its eyes. Its fangs latch into your arm,
pumping venom into your bloodstream.
Within seconds you are unconscious. Not
long afterwards you are dead.

➜ Get back to Chapter 2.

70.

You push the raft off with your hands, but
then have to scurry to jump back on before
it floats away. Your footing slips on the wet
rock and you crash into the shallow water.
It's only when you are in the water and
blood starts to cover your eyes, that you
realise you must have caught your head on
the rock. You feel dizzy and light-headed,
and topple onto the gravel.

➜ You are dead — get back to Chapter 5.

71.

You don't know who this man is, but there's

no way you can outrun a bullet. Slowly, you stop and turn back towards him. The man looks very happy to see you. He shouts, "Don Enrico, por aqui!" then he shoots into the air. Seconds later, you see three more men running towards you. Go to 43.

72.

You move into the faster water and are soon completely out of sight of Enrico. You crash over more whitecap waves. Ramiro almost rolls off at one point, but you use the last of your strength to grab his belt and hold him on. Just when you think you can't hold on any longer, you pass out of the rapids and into calmer water further along the river. Go to 80.

73.

It's easy to follow the tapir's trail through the jungle. You hear the sound of rushing water ahead, and rush forwards as Ramiro hobbles along using his improvised walking stick for support. You come to a sudden stop when you reach the lip of a short drop. To your right, a waterfall plunges into a pool. You turn to help Ramiro when your feet slip from under you. Go to 93.

74.

You turn and wait for Pedro. You dodge the swing of his machette and are just about to lash out with a punch, when he swings the torch up into your face and smashes you across the head with it. The blow knocks you flat on your back. Go to 45.

75.

You decide to wait and see what happens as the other men arrive. The man who looks like the co-pilot is clearly the leader. He talks to Ramiro, and you can see your friend shaking his head. Then the man with the floppy hat points at something in the sand, and the men aim their rifles at the surrounding undergrowth. The man leads

them across the stream. He is tracking you
by following your footprints!

➜   If you want to run away now while
there may be a chance, go to 18.

➜   If you'd prefer to walk out from your
hiding place, go to 50.

76.

Before the guard realises what is
happening, you swing the spade down
and knock him out. You hear someone
shout out your name, and you turn to see
the distinctive shape of Mamani running
into the treeline, pursued by two armed
cocaleros. Suddenly there's the roar of
an turbo-prop engine starting up and a
twin-prop light aeroplane bursts out of the
palm-thatched shed. It has to be Enrico
trying to escape! Without hesitating, you
grab the launcher and snatch a rocket
that has spilled from a bag the guard was
carrying. You easily load the rocket into
place.

➡ If you want to fire the RPG at the men pursuing Mamani, go to 86.

➡ If you want fire the RPG at the twin-prop plane, go to 40.

77.

You throttle the engine up and accelerate towards the forest. The engine whines noisily. Wind buffets your face, forcing tears from your eyes. Whatever you do next, you'd better do it quickly!

→   To pull the control yoke towards you to raise the nose, go to 65.

→   To press the engine cutoff button, go to 21.

78.

You dive down onto the raft and hold on as it lurches through the raging water. A burst of gunfire passes over your head. You hit a wave which spins the raft sideways and into the boulder. The raft snags and slowly rises up on one side. You scream for Ramiro to hang on as you see his body slide into the torrent. Then the raft flips completely and you are thrown into the water. Go to 17.

79.

You grab the spade and manage to knock one guard flat on his back. But the other man swings the butt of his gun down on you and you crash unconscious to the ground. Go to 59.

80.

You hear shouting coming from the rocks above the rapids behind you. The drug-runners knew that the cross on the map meant "rapids", and they did not attempt it in their boat. You survived and are now ahead of them, but you know they will do everything they can to get the satellite phone and map back. You check Ramiro and begin to pole the raft along the river as fast as your aching body will allow.

CHAPTER SIX

It's early afternoon the next day when you reach the airstrip. It's oven hot and you feel you could dry up with thirst. You have left Ramiro hidden down by the river. He has the map, phone and the last of your water, but he is badly injured. If he is discovered by the cocaleros, he will be killed. If you are caught or killed then he will never be found. You know it's a bad situation. So now you sit, hidden in the undergrowth looking out on the airstrip, waiting to see if anyone comes. The airstrip is in a clearing, with longer grass surrounding it. Across the clearing, in the cover of the trees, is Enrico's business operation. There is a camouflaged camp, with several tents, as well as a large, palm-thatched shed, where you can see sacks and other small containers stacked up.

You briefly snooped around there at dawn, but the place was guarded and when a dog started barking you realised that if you didn't get away soon then you would be found. There are at least ten men, and all of them are armed. Enrico arrived a few hours ago, and since then guards have been patrolling the airstrip and surrounding forest every couple of hours.

Survival Challenge: Helicopter Strike

The sun has almost set when you hear the faint "thwacking" noise of helicopter rotor blades. From the sound there are at least two helicopters. The lights in the camp begin to go out one by one. For an instant your spirits lift, but any sense of relief you had at thinking that this is your rescue is shattered when you hear men shouting, "Obtener el arma! Obtener el arma! Disparar a los helicópteros hacia abajo! Rápidamente!" They're going to shoot down the helicopters! Your rescue will be over before it's even begun — and it will be all your fault — you told them to land here!

The decisions you make now will decide whether you live or die.

You have to do something so that the helicopters can land. You don't have much to help you, just the lighter and folding knife, but you do have one advantage — surprise. You get up and put you plan into action.

➜   To start Plan A: quickly move closer to the camp along the trail you followed earlier and set fire to the shed, go to 34.

➜   To start Plan B: light a flaming torch you prepared earlier, then wave it at the incoming helicopters, go to 20.

81.
You decide the best thing to do is stay still. The dangerous-looking snake slowly pans its head up, its forked tongue flicking the air. It pauses, sensing the air, then slowly slides backwards and down the branch.

"We were lucky," Ramiro whispers from behind you. "That was a fer-de-Lance — a deadly pit viper." Go to 46.

82.

You turn the plane again and bank round in a wide turn. The engine temperature alarm is still buzzing. Behind you are mountains and ahead you can see miles of lush rainforest. You can't see the river yet, but you know it's down there somewhere.

➜   If you want to continue searching for the river, go to 96.

➜   If you decide to turn back around and head for the clearing, go to 55.

83.

You dive to the ground. Moments later you hear some screams, and the heavy machine gun falls silent. You don't hang around to find out what happened, and run towards the camp. As you get closer, a man comes out of the darkness. He's holding a rocket-propelled grenade launcher!

➜   If you want to carry out Plan A, and set fire to the shed, go to 28.

➜   If you want to duck down and follow the man holding the RPG, go to 4.

➜   If you want to take cover behind some nearby containers, go to 92.

84.

This way leads you to a spiky tree. Suddenly, there is a shout behind you. You turn to see Pedro lunge at you. He pulls out his gun, and as you grapple with him, it goes off. Only shortly after do you realise you've been hit. You sink to your knees, before you black out forever.

➜   Get back to Chapter 4.

85.

Nothing about the way the man is acting feels right, so you turn to run back the way you came. There is the crack of a rifle shot, and dirt flies up by your feet. The man with the gun shouts, "Paré!"

→ To stop and turn around, go to 71.

→ To ignore the man and keep on running, go to 18.

86.

You look through the sights and fire. The rocket shoots out of the launcher and explodes in front of the guards, knocking them off their feet. They don't get back up. You drop the RPG and grab the guard's handgun as a figure in black runs toward you.

→ To shoot the man in black, go to 67.

→ To drop the gun and hold up your hands, go to 101.

87.

You push on towards the tall trees where

the edge of the swamp must be. You know
there's no sense in going back to the crash
site. The green gloom of the rainforest
closes in around you. The only noises are the
ticking and clicking of hundreds of insects,
and the movement of Ramiro and you
through the water. As you reach the edge of
the swamp, you see a narrow stream.

➜   If you wish to head upstream, go to 1.

➜   To head downstream, go to 66.

88.

You walk over to the tree and lean up
against it briefly, pretending you are
exhausted. You drop the map and phone,
hoping that the men haven't realised what
you were doing. They beckon you over. Go
to 50.

89.

You get back onto the raft where Ramiro
is lying and push off with your pole. You
suddenly hear more gunfire, but you are

88

89

separated from Enrico's boat by a wall of rock. The raft hurtles through the current and you are forced to hold on. Go to 61.

90.
You throttle the engine down, but with less power you have less control — and the plane is still diving towards the ground!

➜ If you want to throttle the engine "up" for more power, go to 77.

➜ If you wish to pull the control yoke towards you, go to 9.

91.
You continue waving the torch, but a bullet shatters your arm and you drop it. Other shots hit home, and you drop down dead.

➜ Stop lying around and get back to Chapter 6!

92.
You take cover behind some containers as more gunfire erupts around you. The

90

91

92

helicopters swoop in over the camp and are taking fire from over by the tents. There is a loud bang and one of the helicopters takes a direct hit from an RPG! It bursts into flames and falls from the sky. Over to your right a man shrieks as he is gunned down — from the outline it looked like he was wearing a floppy bush hat. Whatever you had planned, it wasn't this! The second helicopter closes in and opens fire on the man with the RPG. He's cut down where he stands, but that doesn't help you, as guards appear over to your right and close in on you. It's only then that you notice the containers you are hiding behind are marked "Altamente Flamable".

➜ If you think you could use this to help you, go to 24.

➜ To make a run for it, go to 32.

93.

You crash into the water at the bottom of the waterfall. For a second you flounder in the swirling current, the zip-up bag twisting around you. Then you manage to power up to the surface and take in a deep lungful of air. You haul yourself out onto the rocks alongside the pool.

"Are you OK down there?" Ramiro calls.

You are soaking, but you're alive. "I'm not dead yet!" you shout back. Go to 33.

94.

You push the pole down into the gravel as hard as you can, and force the raft back into the channel leading towards the rapids. Now you can see that if you move quickly, you'll be separated from Enrico's boat by the line of rocks.

➜ To duck down and pole the raft to the left side, where the water is flowing into a seething cauldron of white froth, go to 61.

➜ To keep close to the rocky riverbank where the water is calmer, but slower, go to 38.

95.

You head along the stream and then up onto the flatter ground above the gulley. You help Ramiro up the slope. The undergrowth becomes thicker, and unable to push through, you find yourself heading further away from the water. Something bursts out of the undergrowth with a crash.

A donkey-sized animal with a bristly mane and a short trunk-like nose charges through the bushes, ripping out a trail that heads in the direction of the stream.

➜ If you want to follow the trail made by the tapir, go to 73.

➜ If you wish to continue to find your own way through, go to 15.

➜ If you'd prefer to push back through the undergrowth in the direction of the stream, go to 23.

96.

You continue to press on, but smoke begins to fill the cockpit and without further warning the engine bursts into flames. There's little you can do as the plane plummets down towards the ground where it explodes on impact with a large tree.

➜ You ignored the engine warning light and alarm, and paid the price. Get back to Chapter 1 to try again.

97.

You dive onto your hands and knees leaving the webs above you unbroken. You hope this will be enough to fool your pursuers into thinking you haven't come this way. Once past the webs you can't hear Enrico's men following.

➡ If you want to carry on forward towards a spiky tree trunk, go to 84.

➡ If you want to head over to a large buttress root, go to 62.

98.

The lighthouse tree is probably the best place you'll find to hide the map and phone. You quickly push the items into a gap between the tree's massive roots. You feel happier now they are safely hidden.

➡ If you want to sneak back to where Ramiro is waiting, go to 6.

➡ If you want to walk out to greet the men, go to 50.

99.

About halfway down you hear a ripping noise, and the whole tangle of vines you're climbing down pulls away from the rocks.

➜ To grab another vine, go to 8.

➜ To push yourself away from the cliff and jump into the water, go to 93.

100.

You cut the rope and the camouflage falls down on the guards. You wait to see what happens next. They quickly become tangled in it as they try to get free. They shout out, and another two guards appear. The men quickly spot you, and after a brief chase you're caught and knocked unconscious in the struggle that follows. Go to 59.

101.

You drop the handgun and put your hands up. You are quickly surrounded by Special Operations commandos. You watch as Enrico's plane accelerates up the strip.

You feel cheated by his escape, when suddenly a burst of gunfire leaps out from the side of the helicopter gunship. Enrico's plane cartwheels across the airstrip, before it crashes to a halt in a fireball. The cocaleros are losing the battle now. Some are still firing their guns, but most have fled into the rainforest.

CHAPTER SEVEN

Less than an hour later you're in an army helicopter after picking up Ramiro. The medic tells you that though his injuries are serious, with proper treatment he will make a full recovery.

The army captain checks over Enrico's phone and map.

"Agent Suarez would have been pleased," he shouts over the noise of the

helicopter as you head for the nearest hospital. "We put him undercover on that plane you were on to bust the cocaine cartel."

He shows you a photograph of a smart army officer, who you recognise as Worried Man.

"Thank you," the captain says. "It looks like you have just completed his mission."

**CONGRATULATIONS
YOU HAVE SURVIVED!**

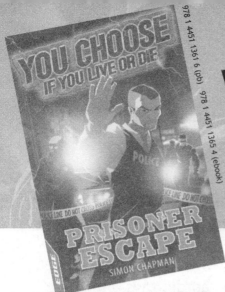